I0004611

The Ultimate Pinterest Guide

by Neo Monefa

Table of Contents

1. What is Pinterest

Pinterest is the newest platform in the social networking block and it's taking the industry by storm. Facebook and Twitter may be the most popular social networking platform today, but Pinterest's success hinges on being different from the rest of the competition. What exactly is Pinterest?

Simply put, Pinterest is a "virtual pinboard." As in a real-life physical pinboard, you will be able to collate and collect images from all over the World Wide Web by pressing the "Pin It" button and assigning it to a pinboard.

The social networking aspect of Pinterest happens on the site itself. Other Pinterest members will be able to see your pinboard and "re-pin" the images on their own pinboards. You can also look at the images and photos that other people has pinned and you will be able to "Love" it, re-pin it or leave a comment. You will also be able to follow other Pinterest members or their individual pinboards to stay up-to-date with the latest images around the Internet.

Pinterest was founded in 2009 and was launched on March 2010. When it was first released, Pinterest was by invitation only and was closed to the public. It was only opened to the general public on

August 10, 2012. Just two years after it was launched, Pinterest now boasts of over 10 million users and this number is expected to grow as there are no more barriers on its registration procedures.

The personal and social side of Pinterest has contributed to its quick and rapid success among individuals. The business and networking side of Pinterest however, is yet to be fully explored by establishments and companies. In this e-book, we will explore the different sides of Pinterest and how you can use it to help your business gain more mileage and exposure.

2. How to Use Pinterest

Before you start pinning and creating unique pinboards on Pinterest, you'll first need to navigate through the site and create your own account. In this section, you will be given a comprehensive step-by-step guide in getting started on Pinterest. You will also learn how to sift through the volume of images on the site to help you browse, "pin" and
"repin" efficiently.
All the information that you will need to get you started on Pinterest is in this chapter.

Creating an Account
When you go to the Pinterest homepage, you will be greeted by a wide variety of images that other Pinterest members find interesting. A comprehensive preview of what's inside Pinterest
Before you can start creating pinboards and pinning images, you will need to create your own Pinterest account. There are three ways to do this: through Facebook, Twitter or your e-mail.
Let's first look at using Facebook to register your Pinterest account. In order to get started, you must be logged in to your Facebook account.
You will see a permissions page that would enable Pinterest to access your information like your e-mail address and the fan pages that you have "Liked" in the past. Click on 'Allow' to continue.
If you want to register using your Twitter account, simply choose the Twitter button from the registration page.
You will be taken to an authorization page where Pinterest will ask for your permission to access information from your Twitter account. Again, you'll need to be logged in to your Twitter account to do this.
After signing into your Twitter account, you will be asked to enter your desired username, your e-mail address and your desired password for your Pinterest account. You will also be able to upload a photo that will be associated with your Pinterest.
The third way to create a Pinterest account is by registering your e-mail address. If you want to keep your other social networking

accounts separate from your Pinterest account, this the way to go. Just click on the right link from the registration page.

After clicking on the link, you will be taken to the page where you will be asked to provide some information about you. You can also upload the photo that you want to associate with your Pinterest account.

When you're done filling out the required fields, click on 'Create Account' to continue.

On the next page, you will be asked to choose five images that you find interesting so that Pinterest will know what types of photos to show you for pinning.

This is the page that you will be directed to after you have registered your account using any of the three methods that we showed you earlier.

Once you have selected the photos that have caught your eye, click on the 'Continue' button to proceed to your Pinterest homepage.

On your first log in, you will see a short note from Pinterest saying that you have to verify your registered e-mail address in order to keep your account active. Check your inbox and spam folder regularly to receive instructions on how to do this.

Now that you have your own Pinterest account, you will be able to pin images that you see on the Internet into your own pinboards. These pinned images will be seen by other Pinterest users and they can also repin them in their own pinboards.

In the next section, we will be exploring what pins and boards are and how you can use them to organize the photos that you want to share to other Pinterest users.

Pins and Boards

Pins and boards are part of what makes Pinterest the visual networking website that it is. The two concepts are the most basic and fundamental parts that makes Pinterest unique.

Let us first look at Boards.

A board is essentially like a folder where you can categorize your pins to follow a certain theme. Like in the example above, the pin is categorized under the 'Admiration' board.

In this example, the Admiration board contains mostly photos of art in different forms, mostly paintings.

Your boards can be about anything that you're interested in. Whether it's DIY projects, fashion, photography or automobiles, the boards will help you organize your interests into one cohesive album.

To create a board, click on the Add + button on the upper right corner of the screen.

A prompt will give you three options. Simply select 'Create a Board' to get started.

On the next prompt that you'll see, you will be able to set the name of your board, its category and the people who has the permission to pin images to that board.

The board name can be any word or phrase that you want. It can be something as specific as "Wedding Ideas" or "Funny Pictures" to something generic like "Things That Make Me Glad".

After you type in the board name that you want, you will need to choose a board category.

In the example above, we chose to make a board just for cute animal photos. In the board category, the most accurate option is obviously 'Animals' so we will go with that.

You also have the option to allow other people to contribute pins to the board. You can add names of the people you follow on Pinterest. Simply type in the first few letters of their name and choose the right person from the auto-generated names that will appear.

When you're done adding, click on the 'Add' button.

If you're satisfied with the settings of the board, click on 'Create Board' to continue.

You can always edit the settings of your board at any time. To do this, go to the board that you want to edit and then click on the 'Edit Board' button.

When you find an image that you want to place on a board, all you'll need to do is to pin it. There are several ways to do it.

But first things first, what is a pin?

Essentially, a "pin" is an image that you want to share to other Pinterest users. It can be any image that you took yourself or stumbled upon on the Internet or around Pinterest. A pin is a reflection of your visual taste, interests, likes and hobbies.

You can use the 500 characters to cite the source of the image or you can talk about what you like about the photo.

It is very easy to pin an image on Pinterest. Just hover your mouse pointer on the image that you like and then click the 'Repin' button. When you pin an image on Pinterest, you can include a short, 500-character description about the photo which other Pinterest users will be able to see.

If you noticed, above the description box there's a dropdown menu. This is where you can choose which board you want to pin an image to.

The last step is to click the 'Pin It' button and the image will be visible on the board it was pinned to.

Another way to add an image to a board is to click on a Pinterest icon on a website where the image is found.

After clicking on the Pinterest icon, a popup window will appear. Here, you will be able to choose the board you want to pin it to and change or add a description to the photo.

When you're done editing the settings, click on 'Pin It' to make the pin appear on the board you selected.

Some websites do not have a Pinterest icon for their images but it's still possible to pin those photos. The first step is to click on the 'Add +' link on the upper right hand side of your Pinterest homepage. This is the same button that you will click if you were to create a board like we did earlier.

This time however, select 'Add a Pin'.

After selecting 'Add a Pin', you will see another prompt where you will enter the URL the page where your image is located.

Pinterest will auto generate the images on that page. Scroll through the images to find the one that you want to put on your board.

Select the board you want the image pinned to and include a short description of the image. When you're done, click on the 'Pin It' button.

If the pinning was successful, you will be taken to the pin's page.

The third way to pin an image to your board is to upload it from your files. Again, we will begin by clicking on the 'Add +' button but this time, choose the 'Upload Pin' option.

The next prompt will allow you to choose the image from your files. After you have chosen the photo that you want to pin, choose the board that you want to pin it to and add a short description about the photo.

If the upload was successful, you will be directed to the pin's page. From here, other Pinterest users will be able to see and repin the photo. They can also "Like" it or leave comments.

There are hundreds of photos that are pinned to Pinterest at any given time. One way to sift through the massive volume of images is to focus on the images that were pinned by your contacts and direct connections.

Adding Contacts

One of Pinterest's similarities with Twitter is that people can "Follow" your posts, pins and boards and you can also follow other people's pins and boards. This is a great way to organize the pins that you will see on Pinterest. At any given time, you can see hundreds of pins on Pinterest. Filtering the pins to just the ones posted by the people that you follow will ensure that what you see is relevant to what you like.

It is easy to add and friends to follow on Pinterest. Just hover on the upper right corner where your name and photo is located.

First, let's look at the 'Invite Friends' option.

When you click on the 'Invite Friends' link, you will be directed to the page where you can choose between the different ways that you can invite friends.

The first option is for you to manually input the e-mail addresses of the contacts that you want to invite. You can also add a personal note that they will see when they receive the invitation from Pinterest.

You can also invite your friends on Facebook to join Pinterest if they don't have an account yet. You can also follow your friends that are already on Pinterest.

The next option is to use your Gmail account to retrieve your address book. Pinterest assures that no invitations or e-mails will be sent out without your approval.

Before you can use your Gmail account to send invites, you will need to be logged into your account and give Pinterest permission to retrieve your address book. A popup window will appear. Click on 'Allow Access' to continue.

Once you have allowed Pinterest access to your Gmail address book, you will be directed to two lists of your contacts on the main window. As in adding friends on Facebook, you can begin following your contacts that already have a Pinterest account.

For your contacts that have yet to create their Pinterest accounts, the 'Invite' button will send an invitation to their e-mails with instructions on how to register an account.

The last option is to use your Yahoo! mail account to search for contacts. As in Gmail, you will be asked to log in to your account and allow Pinterest to access your address book.

A popup window will appear. Click on the 'Agree' button to continue.

As in Gmail, you will see a list of your contacts that are not yet on Pinterest, as well as the ones who are. Follow the ones who already have a Pinterest account and send an invitation to your contacts whom you want to interact with on the site.

Now that you are following people, it will be easier to sift through the volume of images on Pinterest. In the next section, we will be looking at the different ways that you can search or browse through pinned photos on Pinterest.

Browsing on Pinterest

Browsing on Pinterest can be overwhelming because of the sheer volume of images that greet you at any given time. Even on your account's homepage, you can already begin browsing photos from around the Internet, or just review the images that you have pinned. Let's first look at the different parts of your homepage.

As you can see from the screenshot above, there is a lot happening on the homepage. The pins that you'll see in your homepage are the images that you have pinned on your board, as well as images that were pinned by the people you follow.

The column on the left details the activity of your pins and boards. In this column, you will see the names of other Pinterest users who have "repinned" your pin or has started following one of your boards.

At the top of the page, you will see the main browsing menu or options.

The default homepage view shows the pins of the people you follow. You have several options to choose from if you want to look at other pins that other Pinterest users have pinned.

The first option is to browse by category. Simply hover on the 'Categories' link on the menu at the top of the page. A dropdown menu will show the different categories that photos are placed into. Just click on the category that you want to browse and your homepage will be filled with photos from that category. For example, clicking on the Animals category will give you all the most recent pins of other Pinterest users.

Pinterest automatically fetches pins when you get to the bottom of the page. Endless scrolling is used when browsing through Pinterest so you won't have to click on links to go to other pages.

Another way to browse pins is by clicking on the 'Everything' link from the menu bar.

Here, the photos that you'll see are random and from all categories. If you're looking to simply browse and enjoy photos of all topics, this is the best way to explore Pinterest.

The next browsing tip is to select 'Popular' from the menu.

As the title suggests, here you will find the most repinned and liked pins on Pinterest.

You can also use Pinterest to browse for products being sold online. Choose the 'Gifts' link from the menu bar to see a catalogue of products posted on Pinterest.

When you hover over the link, you will see a dropdown menu of the different price ranges. Choose the price range of your budget.

It should be noted however that the items are not sold within Pinterest. The images are also external links to the product pages and websites of the people or companies that sell them.

The prices of the products can be easily seen, a nifty feature that makes it easier for shoppers to find what they're looking for budget-wise.

Browsing Pinterest need not be an overwhelming experience. With the simple browsing tips that we provided in this section, you will be able to peruse the most interesting photos on the World Wide Web. In the next section we will look at some advanced tips that you can use to make every Pinterest moment memorable. These tips will make it easier for you to post pins on your boards and to organize your pins into a constructive and efficient album.

Advanced Pinterest Tips

One of the most appealing things about Pinterest is its limitless potential. Words take a backseat on Pinterest as photos and images take center stage. There are times however when too much visuals can overwhelm the senses. With the sheer volume of images on Pinterest, it can be daunting to sort through all of them without getting exhausted. In this section, we will look at some tips that will make browsing images on Pinterest an enjoyable affair.

Install browser extensions and add-ons

Whether you're using Firefox, Chrome, Safari or any other Internet browser, the best way to easily pin images that you on the web is to download and install add-ons and/or extensions specifically designed to make pinning a breeze.

Here are some of the most popular and efficient add-ons for Firefox and Chrome:

• Pinterest-Right-Click for Firefox allows you to right-click on an image and choose the 'Pin It' option from your standard menu. A popup box will appear where you will be able to choose the board you want to pin it to, as well as write in the standard description box.

• Pinterest Pro for Chrome allows you to right-click on an image to pin it to your board. It also makes browsing on Pinterest easier as it automatically zooms into the full-size pin from your homepage so you won't need to click on an image to see the regular size.

• Screen 2 Pin for Chrome lets you upload screenshots of an entire web page with just one click.

• Pinterest Recent Activity Expander is the standalone version of your Recent Activity column. It will show you thumbnails of your pins that were repinned, as well your new followers.

Use hashtags

Just like in Twitter, hashtags can be used in Pinterest to make searching for themes, topics and subjects a lot easier. To do this, simply add a "#" before a word in the description of the pin. If you want to ensure maximum exposure for your pin, make sure that your hashtags are broad enough to make it easier for people to see your pin when they make a search.

Take advantage of Pinterest's "Goodies"

Pinterest offers a bookmarklet that will make it easier for you to pin photos from the Internet without having to go to the website. Their Goodies page also has other free tools for bloggers, website owners and smartphone users.

Tag your friends in your pins

Pinterest is a social site after all. If you come across a pin that you think your friend, someone you're following or one of your followers will appreciate, simply tag their names on your pin description. To do this, just type "@" followed by your friend's name.

Add a price tag to your pins

Whether you're pinning a handmade earring that you found on Etsy or your own products for sale, it will be very useful for you to include the price in your product description so that other pinners will already know the cost without having to search for the item elsewhere. It will also let other Pinterest users know that the item is for sale because it will appear on the 'Gifts' section of Pinterest. The price will appear as a sort of sash on the left-hand corner of the pin.

To add a price for your pin, simply type in the price on the pin description field. Don't forget to add the "$" sign before the price.

Update the photo cover of your boards

When other Pinterest users visit your page, they will see your profile and your boards. If you want other users to follow you, use your board's covers to entice them to do so. You can choose any of the pins that you have assigned to your boards. Choose a visually appealing photo that encapsulates the main idea of the board. Also ensure that the photo will look good on the cover itself. Because of the size of the board covers, the angle of a photo may not be suited to be a cover photo. This may take some trial and error but your effort will not go to waste.

Angles are awkward and the covers are not appealing.

The photos are optimized for the cover and they give a good visual description of the pins inside.

Make your boards more specific

One of the objectives of Pinterest is to make it easy for its users to find the photo that they need. This purpose is often defeated by pinners who have over a multitude of boards with over a hundred pins each. Trying to find something specific like a photo of cupcakes in a board that has photos of all types of desserts and pastries can be exhausting.

Even if you only have 10 pins of the same topic (cupcakes, for example), it will be better for you to provide those pins with its own board. This will also make it easier for you to find images that you have pinned from a year ago. You can make boards of specific areas of interest like DIY Hair Accessories or Must-Try Christmas Recipes. The possibilities are as endless as your creativity.

Rearrange your boards

If you are planning to have seasonal boards (Christmas, Valentines, etc.) you will want those boards to be highlighted at the appropriate time. To do this, you will need to rearrange your boards to make your profile look sensible and up-to-date.

To do this, go to your profile page by clicking on your icon at the upper right hand corner of the page. Once your profile is right in front of you, click on the "rearrange boards" icon.

Having no specific board order makes your profile confusing. It is difficult to promote boards that you want other people to see or follow.

After clicking on the icon, simply drag and drop the boards to your preferred order. When you're done, click on the check mark to save the arrangement.

The four boards about Halloween are in the middle of the page, making it the first boards that profile visitors will see. The Inspiration and Admiration boards are on each side to make the arrangement more coherent. You can also change the cover photo of the boards to make the view more cohesive.

Now that you know how to make your profile more appealing to visitors, it's time to start pinning and adding photos to your boards. One of the biggest pet peeve in Pinterest however is the pinning of low-quality photos that are often flagged as spam or inappropriate. In the next section, we will look at different tips that you can use to ensure that you only contribute and upload high-quality and relevant photos to Pinterest.

What to Pin on Pinterest

It is very tempting to post every single photo that you adore on Pinterest, especially with browser tools and add-ons that make pinning extremely convenient. Some images however are not meant to be pinned. In this section, we will look at the guideline to Pinterest pinning and what images will make a good pin.

Before pinning a photo, answer these basic questions to determine whether it's a pin that would contribute to the quality of your page or not.

Is picture quality good?

Take a moment to browse around Pinterest and you may notice that 90% of the photos are of a decent resolution and are not pixilated. That's because other Pinterest members take their time in searching for images that are Pinterest-worthy. Not all photos are created equal, and not all photos deserve to be on Pinterest.

If you need to pull out a photo editing software like Adobe Photoshop to improve its quality, you can certainly do so. Just make sure that you credit the image source when you pin it.

Is the photo appropriate or offensive?

It is very tempting to post photos that may be humorous to us but offensive to others. After all, what's funny isn't the same for everybody else. Before you pin an image to one of your boards, ask yourself first if it can be offensive to others. Does the image poke fun at someone else? Does it discriminate? Better to be sure than to receive negative comments on your pin or be flagged by Pinterest for not following their guidelines.

Opt for constructive photos rather than the offensive. Your followers and other Pinterest users will love you for it.

Will other people be able to relate to your pin?

Remember that even if Pinterest is considered as a social networking site, you have very little opportunity to describe in words your interests and personal life. Pinterest is powered by pins and photos. For other people to understand the person behind the profile, they will need to understand what your photo is trying to convey.

To this end, family photos that are neither artistic nor memorable are discouraged from being pinned. You can post those photos on Facebook but not on Pinterest. The same goes to self-portraits that do not introduce a novel or unique idea to the public.

Is it unique and interesting?
A lot of people become addicted to Pinterest because of the quality of the pins that they see. It is different from simply browsing images on Google Images, for example. On Pinterest, they know that the photo that they will see is something extraordinary and hard to find. Catalogue-like photos are also discouraged on Pinterest. One of the most important goals of Pinterest is to promote and encourage creativity and individuality. If you think that the photo that you are considering to pin looks blah and generic, best leave it where it is.

Is it something that people will want to buy or do?
Use your Pinterest boards to inspire other people, whether it's to purchase a unique and useful product or to spend an afternoon crafting a one-of-a-kind creation. While Pinterest is slowly becoming an essential marketing tool for businesses and establishments, the pins still need to be creative and inspiring. If you find a photo around the Internet that you yourself will purchase or do on a weekend, post it on one of your boards and tag a friend to buy or make it with you.

It is not difficult to get used to pinning images to your Pinterest boards. What may take some practice however is knowing which images to pin and which ones to avoid. Take your time in browsing and repinning pins on Pinterest to get a good idea of the types of photos that are posted in each of your category of interest, as well as the quality of the photos pinned.

You should also take the time to learn more about Pinterest's pinning guidelines or "Pin Etiquette." The people who use Pinterest make the high-quality visual networking site that it is. The community will not hesitate to report you if you have posted an offensive and distasteful image.

Your interaction with other pinners should also be respectful. Though from time to time you may see comments that are downright mean and rude, it doesn't mean that you should participate in the same form of criticism. If you want to have and maintain a good standing in Pinterest, you will need to watch what you say and offer constructive criticisms on the pins that you want to comment on. Images aren't the only type of pins that can be found on Pinterest. You can also pin videos from YouTube and Vimeo. This is especially helpful if you are running a marketing campaign on Pinterest because it allows you to share your commercials, promo videos and other related videos with the Pinterest community. In the next section, you will learn how to pin videos on Pinterest and what strategies you can use to make pinners watch your pins.

Pinning Videos on Pinterest
It might surprise you to know that you can also pin videos on Pinterest. It is a new feature that Pinterest recently launched and has been a favorite of millions of users from all over the world.
If a photo is not enough to send your message across, a video just might do the trick. Unfortunately, Pinterest can only pin videos from YouTube and Vimeo or videos that you upload directly from your system.
Follow these steps to pin a video from YouTube or Vimeo.
Click on the 'Add +" button at the upper right hand of your screen which will bring you to the add a new pin or board dialogue box. Choose the 'Add a Pin' option.
Enter the URL of the YouTube or Vimeo video and then click on the 'Find Images' button.
Pinterest will automatically fetch the video from YouTube or Vimeo and will include a thumbnail which also doubles as a link to its source. Choose the board you want to pin the video to and add a short description of the video.
Click on the 'Pin It' button when you're ready to pin the video.
To upload your own video, choose the 'Upload a Pin' option from the 'Add +' popup box. Browse your files for the video that you want to upload. It may take some time before the video is fully uploaded depending on the size of your file.
Add your video description and choose the board you want to pin it to.
Wait until the thumbnail is completely visible before you hit the 'Pin It' button.

Your followers and other Pinterest users will be able to see, like, comment on and repin your video if they find it interesting. Remember to use hashtags to make your video easy to search for.

It is that easy to upload a video to Pinterest. For best results, upload compact videos that are reasonably sized to cut your upload time in half.

This feature is extremely useful for uploading marketing videos and other advertising materials to promote businesses, promos and companies. In the next chapter, we will go in-depth with the different ways that Pinterest can help a business or establishment gain a loyal following using creative images and catchy videos.

3. Using Pinterest for Your Business

Pinterest may have initially started as a personal social networking site but just like Facebook and Twitter, businesses, brands and companies have realized the potential of Pinterest for their marketing and advertising needs. In this chapter, we will explore the different ways that Pinterest can help drive traffic to your website, promote your products and services and help you gain a legion of loyal followers that you can rely on to help your bottom line.

Using Pinterest for Marketing

Because Pinterest is 95% visual, you will need to grab the user's attention using creative, unique and catchy images. This can be a challenge for a lot of startups and SMEs that may not have the marketing budget to hire professional photographers or digital artists to help them produce the type of images that will get mileage on Pinterest.

Even without professional photos, you can still use Pinterest to your business' advantage. Here are some tips to guide you on your Pinterest marketing campaign:

•   Use your other social networking accounts to promote your Pinterest page. Regularly post and promote your Pinterest page on your company's Facebook and Twitter accounts to let your followers know that you are also posting content on other platforms. Remember that Pinterest is also a great way to find new customers and leads so be sure that people know how to find you there.

•   Pay attention to the content that you post on Pinterest. Before Pinterest users read the description of your photo, the photo itself needs to catch their attention first. Pay close attention to the quality, topic and relevance of your pins to ensure that people will want to repin it on their own boards. Do not limit yourself to just product photos. If you use a creative packaging method or if you have unique flyers that you hand out, you can pin high quality photos of those too.

- Use online tools to search for images. If you run out of original content to post, it doesn't mean that your Pinterest campaign must be sacrificed. There are several online tools that are effective in helping you find images that are relevant to your other pins.

If you are using Google Chrome as your Internet browser, download and install PinSearch. It is a free plug-in that will allow you to search for relevant and similar photos on Pinterest. For Firefox browsers, the add-on TinEye will let you do a quick Google search of similar photos by right-clicking the photo and choosing the TinEye function from the menu.
If you prefer to do your image search without installing additional functionalities, you can use Google Images. Just click on the camera icon on the search bar. Upload your base photo and Google with search for similar images on the
Internet.

- Get to know the influential pinners on Pinterest. There are Pinterest users who have a large number of followers, making them influential and effective for your Pinterest marketing campaign. Research on and identify these pinners using online tools like PinReach. These tools often include analytics on Pinterest pages, use it to study your own page to know how you can improve the ranking of your profile. Reach out to the top pinners that are relevant to your topic. Engage them offline and even offer them care packages for helping your campaign.

- Direct traffic back to your website. There's only so much information that you can provide on Pinterest with its limited 500-character pin description. Instead of relying on Pinterest to sell your products, you can use it as a tool to get people to your website where they can learn more about you, your business and the products that you sell. Use boards to highlight some of your products and how buyers will be able to use it. Create a Lifestyle Board or seasonal boards to show your products in action. This will be an effective technique to generate interest for your products and drive customers to your website where they can make a purchase.

We have an entire section dedicated to driving traffic to your website which you will see later on.

•   Make it easy for your website visitors to pin your photos. By simply adding the 'Pin It' button, visitors of your website will be able to pin images that they find interesting to their own boards. Installing a Pinterest button is quick and easy. This simple act has helped hundreds of businesses get their products seen by thousands of people. It also helps in directing pinners to your website where they can see more photos or get a better idea of your company.

•   Monitor and evaluate information. As in any online marketing campaign, you will need the help of analytics to make sense of the progress of your campaign. Check which types of images are the most effective in bringing traffic to your website and pin more of these types of images. Use analytics to determine what kind improvements can be implemented on your Pinterest marketing campaign.

•   Upload or pin videos. Pinterest now allows video pins from YouTube and Vimeo. This is an excellent way to engage with pinners if photos are not enough to spread your message. If you have a YouTube channel or Vimeo account for your business, these video pins can be used to link to the page where they can watch more videos about your products.

•   Use quotes with relevant images. If you browse through Pinterest, you may notice that there are quite a number of quotations and statements juxtaposed with blurred background images being pinned and repinned. This is currently the most popular trend on Pinterest and if you want your marketing campaign to succeed, you will need to post the type of images that are guaranteed to be repinned.

An example would be to use photos of your products as the background and use quotes that would promote it. Let's say that your main product is customized modern living room furniture, you should choose a quotation that promotes relaxation or home aesthetics.

You don't need Photoshop skills in order to create your own text on image pins. You can simply use PinWords to do the work for you. It is a free service that is very easy to use. Just upload your image, choose a text template and type in your quote. You can automatically pin it to your board from the site when you're done.

• Engage your audience. Ensure that commenting is allowed for the pins that you post so that other Pinterest users can give you feedback on your products. You also need to make it a point to reply to the comments that other users leave on your pins. This is a great way to talk about your product or to research your market. Customers will also appreciate your personal approach to their comments and questions.

Businesses and companies are just now realizing the potential of Pinterest in their marketing campaigns. If done right, your Pinterest campaign can generate hundreds of new leads which can translate to hundreds of new customers. Plan your Pinterest campaign carefully and use it to complement your other online marketing projects.

Branding on Pinterest

Another useful function of Pinterest is to help get your brand recognized by as many people as possible. It can be a tall order to get your brand to the right market but with Pinterest, even minimal effort can go a long way.

The demographics of Pinterest will make you want to consider it for your online branding campaign. A whopping 80% of Pinterest users are female, 50% of which have kids. The age group that is the most active on Pinterest belongs to the 23 to 34 bracket.

When it comes to businesses and the retail industry, Pinterest users follow an average of 9.3 retailers compared to only 6.9 for Facebook users and 8.5 for Twitter users and they spend up to 70% more on Pinterest referrals as compared to non-social referrals.

These statistics make Pinterest a goldmine for branding. If you are able to plan and execute your campaign flawlessly, you will be able to translate pins and repins to sales and active leads. If you are considering using Pinterest for your branding campaign, follow these guidelines to maximize your efforts:

•   Review your brand and social media marketing strategy to see whether a Pinterest branding campaign will be appropriate for your goals. It may seem like a simplistic approach but remember, Pinterest is not for everyone. If you are selling plumbing supplies or cleaning services, you will need to augment your strategy to make it fit the format of Pinterest. If you are able to translate your products into relatable images, Pinterest can definitely make it worth your while.

•   Appeal to the users' emotions. An artistic or high resolution photo is not enough to get your message across. You will need to engage the users' emotions to get them to repin, like or comment on your photo. Before pinning anything on your boards, review whether the image will elicit an emotional response. You will need to be more creative when taking and posting photos of your products. A photo of a coffee table with a plain, white background will not get you far, for example. A photo of a coffee table in a well lighted living room with other home décor on the other hand will get a better response.

•   Always ensure that the photos that you post convey high quality. If you are trying to sell a product, a low resolution generic photo will not do it justice. You will to encapsulate unique features, selling points and premium quality in a single photograph. Bear in mind that Pinterest users see hundreds of pins at any given time. Your pins need to standout from the rest of the pins and grab the users' interest.

•   Make it a point to only post the photos that will strongly and positively reflect your brand. You do not want your brand to be associated with anything that you are not proud of. Pin carefully and thoughtfully.

•   Pin images that are concrete and easy to understand. You want your audience to immediately know what the pin is all about without having to take a second to understand what it means. Abstract pins may be pleasing to the eye but it cannot send a clear message. If your brand and products deal need a more straightforward approach, only pin images that will suit your purpose.

•   Use a "call to action" on your pins. A call to action is words or phrases that urge the audience to do something. Phrases like "Click here" or "Check it out" are some of the most familiar call to action statements on the Internet. On Pinterest, users are 80% more likely to respond to a call to action than other social media platforms. It is easy to produce tacky graphics with call to action statements highlighted on the image. In Pinterest, these types of pins are not very appealing.

You will need to come up with a clever and creative way to encourage users to do what you want them to do. Whether it's to visit your website or repin your pin, the call to action must be clear yet elegant. Here are some examples:

•   Use viral media. Whether its photos or videos, if you want your brand to reach the widest audience possible, look to memes and popular content to get your message across. Use catchy statements and witty catchphrases juxtaposed on appropriate images to make users want to repin your pins to their followers. Pinterest is a great tool in reaching audiences from all over the country, even all over the world. As long as you pin the right type of viral images and/or videos, your branding campaign will be a success.

• Let your personality shine through. At the end of the day, you are your brand and there is no one in the world who best understands your brand than you. Make sure that every image that you pin on Pinterest reflects your brand, and by extension, you. Use your pins to introduce your brand to people and to make it easy for them to remember you.

• Don't just focus on the products, associate your products to a lifestyle that they can relate to or aspire for. Post tips, suggestions and inspiration to your followers to make them anticipate your pins. This is also a great way to get your audience to associate your brand to a certain way of life or persona.

Branding in itself is a big challenge that all businesses must face at some point. Pinterest makes it very easy for you to reach millions of people by pinning relevant, creative and up-to-date photos that reflect your brand most accurately.

In the next section we will look at the different tools that you can use to monitor the performance of your Pinterest marketing or branding campaign. Analytics is an important aspect in any online marketing campaign and Pinterest is no different. With the right tools, you will be able to pinpoint the areas that need improvement and the habits that you need to keep doing.

Driving Traffic From Pinterest

One of the most important functions of Pinterest in an online marketing campaign is to direct traffic from pins into websites. As mentioned before, there's only so much that a pin can say with its 500-character description. If you want your audience to learn more about your products, services and brand, they need to go to your website.

With the right type of pins and pinning strategy, you will be able to utilize Pinterest in successfully driving traffic to your website or blog. Follow the tips that you will see in this section to know how.

• Create your own pinning ratio. There's a lot of debate on whether you should pin your own images or not when it comes to Pinterest online marketing. Most experts agree that both your own and somebody else's images should used if you are looking to Pinterest to drive traffic to your website.

There is no optimal set ratio for pinning content so you may need to go through some trial and error to discover the best ratio for your campaign. In the next section, we will show you a list of monitoring tools that will be essential in determining your own pinning ration.

You can also create specific boards highlighting your own images that you have uploaded. This is a good way to organize your pins so that your followers will be easily updated of any new pins that you have posted.

• Be vigilant. For your Pinterest marketing and branding campaign to be successful, you will need to spend a lot of time on the site, not only pinning and commenting, but also to ensure that images or pins that belong to you link back
to your site. You can guarantee that if you upload high-quality and creative images as pins, other Pinterest users will repin it to their own boards.

Your pins will not get its deserved mileage if the repins do not link back to your site. To avoid this, send a friendly note to the pinner and request for them to link your site. Send them your link to make it easy and convenient for them and thank them for appreciating your images. This is also a great way for you to reach out to your audience beyond Pinterest.

• Take pride in your follower count. After you have built a substantial following on Pinterest, be sure to let your suppliers, business contacts and network know. Include your follower count on media kits, brochures and business cards. You can also highlight the number on your website or blog. You don't need to be specific with the number of followers that you have since you may be adding more each day. Feel free to round up to the nearest hundreds.

•   Enrich your board with keywords. The best way to get your pins found is to use keywords on your board title and description. This will make it easier for your boards to show up in search results. You can use Google's Keyword Tool, which is free for keyword research.

•   Include your website's URL wherever possible. Be it on your profile or pin description, be sure to mention your website whenever you can. This is an effective way to stamp the URL in your audience's mind. It will be easier for them to know more about your brand if they are able to go to your website without taking cues from links.

•   Use text-rich images. Even if Pinterest is a visual platform, you don't have to strictly pin only photos. In fact, you can use a relevant quotation or statement as your main image with an abstract background. Text images have risen in popularity in Pinterest and if your audience can relate to the statement on the photo, rest assured that they will repin it.

This is also helpful if you don't have a lot of pictures to work with. With the right statement, your pin will make its rounds on hundreds of pinners' boards.

•   Use Pinterest as a research tool. You can also use Pinterest to research other pins that use similar keywords as yours. If they get a lot of repins, likes or comments, you may need to start taking notes and use their format as inspiration for your own content. Pinterest is also a great starting point in discovering what people are talking about now. Just spin these topics and find a unique angle that you can use for your own campaign.
•   Use the seasons to your advantage. There are millions of Pinterest users who use the site to research on creative holiday decors, gifts and other ideas. Capitalize on your audience's interest by creating seasonal boards and pinning relevant images. To make

posting more efficient, plan ahead. Create an editorial calendar for the whole year and post blogs and other website updates to coincide with your pins.

•   Add "stickiness" to your site. You will need to stay on top of your Pinterest campaign and monitor the amount of clicks, repins, likes and comments that you get for each post. Analyze the information that you have to determine which pins and topics get the most traction. Follow up on these pins by posting something relevant.

For example, if you notice that a specific recipe that you posted gets the most views and repins, simply post a modified recipe that is similar to the first.

•   Give your followers something just for them. Create exclusive boards that only your followers will have access to. This will encourage other Pinterest users to follow you as well. You may post exclusive coupons, news and updates or a sneak peek to your products.

•   Collaborate with your followers. A useful Pinterest feature that you can take advantage of is allowing your followers to post pins on your boards. Create boards that would let them put their own input and creativity to the test. You can hold exclusive contests and give an award to the best or most liked pin. This technique will bridge a gap between you and your followers. It will be good for your Pinterest campaign because it encourages people to follow you to get a chance to get involved with similar activities.

Pinterest has so much potential in driving traffic to your website. There are now millions of Pinterest users worldwide. With the right campaign strategy, you will be able to take advantage of this volume to create awareness and interest for your brand and the products and/or services that you offer.

Tools for Monitoring Your Pinterest Campaign

Any marketing campaign whether it's done offline or online needs to be monitored so that you will have a better understanding of its effectiveness. Fortunately, there are a number of good and accurate monitoring tools for Pinterest campaigns and we will explore the five best ones in this section.

PinReach
http://www.pinreach.com/

PinReach is a monitoring and analytics tool specifically made for Pinterest pages. This tool not only tells you of your campaign's performance, it also showcases trending pins and pinners. This will give an idea of who to follow or reach out to for your campaign, as well as the type of content that users are currently repinning on their board.

It is a free service that has been featured on popular Internet sites such as Mashable and Huffington Post. To register, all you will need to do is to give your Pinterest URL and some basic information. You will be able to see the score of your post and which of your pins are the most popular to Pinterest users.

Repinly
http://www.repinly.com/

Repinly is similar to PinReach but is not as innovative. If you want basic, no-frills analytics, Repinly can give you the information that you need. You will be able to look at the most popular pins on Pinterest at a given time, as well as the most influential Pinterest users. When creating an account, you can choose to register with your Facebook or Twitter account. You will be asked to provide your Pinterest username and you can include up to five tags to associate with your profile.

Repinly also has a scoring system based on the account's popularity, activity and influence. The highest score that a Pinterest profile can get is 100. You can also access statistics gathered by Repinly which detail the activities of the Pinterest population. These stats can be used in crafting or planning your Pinterest campaign.

Pinerly

http://www.pinerly.com

Pinerly is your one-stop Pinterest campaign destination. In order for Pinerly to track your metrics, your campaign must begin and thrive through the website. You will be able to see the number of clicks that your pins receive, the times when the pin was clicked and other important information that can help your fine tune your campaign. Pinerly will also suggest sites, content and images that are relevant to your campaign. This will give you more time to interact with your followers without sacrificing content-hunting for you boards.

As of the moment, Pinerly is not yet open to the public. There is a waitlist for new registrations. To make your registration get approved faster, you are encouraged to share a unique Pinerly URL that will be provided to your friends, family and other followers on other social networking sites.

Cyfe
http://www.cyfe.com

Cyfe is an all-in-one analytics tool for all your social media campaigns, including Pinterest. There is a paid version which has more features, but for a basic Pinterest marketing campaign, the free version is more than enough. To sign up, simply provide your full name and your e-mail address. You will be sent a verification link to the e-mail that you provided. Click on the link and you will be automatically logged into your Cyfe dashboard.

The limitation for the free version however makes Cyfe an incomplete monitoring tool. It simply lists and summarizes the activity on your Pinterest account. You won't get a complete look at the performance of your campaign. If you simply want a tool that will summarize the activity on all your social networking campaigns, Cyfe can give you those metrics.

Pinpuff
http://pinpuff.com/

Pinpuff is a simple tool that will calculate the influence of your Pinterest account. There is no need to sign up or register in order to see your "Pinfluence" score. From the homepage, just type out your e-mail address and provide your Pinterest username.

You will also receive a Pinfluence Score Report that details your reach, activity and "virality" score. Each board will also be scored based on the number of followers of the boards, its pins, repins and likes. Pinpuff is still working on its algorithm so scores for individual pins are still unavailable. All in all, Pinpuff is a useful tool that you can use alongside other tools mentioned earlier.

Analytics and monitoring tools are essential in keeping tabs with your Pinterest campaign. This will help you improve areas that are underperforming and let you know what you need to continue doing. Feel free to test out all the tools mentioned in this section to find which site you are most comfortable with. You may need to use more than one tool in order to get all the information that you will need for your campaign.

4. Enjoy Pinterest

Pinterest has become an influential social networking platform. Even in the absence of lengthy and wordy personal descriptions, Pinterest has thrived as a personal social media site. Photos and videos take center stage on Pinterest as its users pin and repin images from all over the Internet. It has become a haven for DIY and arts and crafts fanatics, as well as wedding planners, fashionistas and photography enthusiasts.

Pinterest has also become a useful and effective online marketing tool for businesses and establishments. If you are a business owner or a marketing professional, you should definitely consider running a Pinterest campaign for your products and/or services.

The demographics of Pinterest offer a glimpse of its potential for marketing and advertising. A Pinterest user spends an average of an hour and 17 minutes browsing through the site. Pinterest users are also more likely to purchase a product that was recommended by their contacts on the site. If you are able to plan and execute a successful marketing campaign on Pinterest, you will be able to reach your sales goals in record speed.

Pinterest is also useful in driving traffic to your website. Images are great for catching one's attention and on Pinterest, excellent images are not only clicked, they are shared with other Pinterest users. The pins that you upload on Pinterest should be externally linked to a page on your website or the homepage itself. If the user finds your pin interesting, they will want to know more about what they are seeing. Make sure that your pins follow the same theme as your website. This way, your Pinterest boards will be seen more as an extension of your site rather than just another social networking platform.

You can also use Pinterest to create catalogs of your products. This is a creative and effective way to highlight your products and to engage your audience. This technique can easily help translate comments and repins to sales, especially if you join in on the conversations on your pins.

To measure the success and shortcomings of your Pinterest campaign, you can utilize free tools that are available online. These tools will help you gauge the types and degree of adjustments that you will need to make in order to improve your campaign's performance.

All in all, Pinterest can greatly help your online marketing campaign. If done right, your Pinterest campaign can help you generate new leads, drive traffic to your website and promote your business, brand and products to thousands of potential customers.

5. THANK YOU FOR READING!

Thank You so much for reading this book. If this title gave you a ton of value, It would be amazing for you to leave a <u>REVIEW</u> !

THANK YOU FOR DOWNLOADING! IF YOU ENJOYED THIS BOOK AND WOULD LIKE TO READ MORE TITLES FROM MY COLLECTION CLICK THIS LINK